I Take C… My Dog

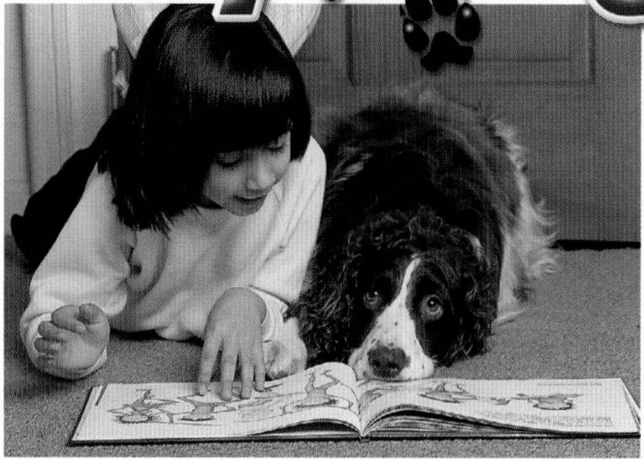

Sophia Loughrey
Photographs by Tom Lippert

Rigby®
A Harcourt Achieve Imprint

www.Rigby.com
1-800-531-5015

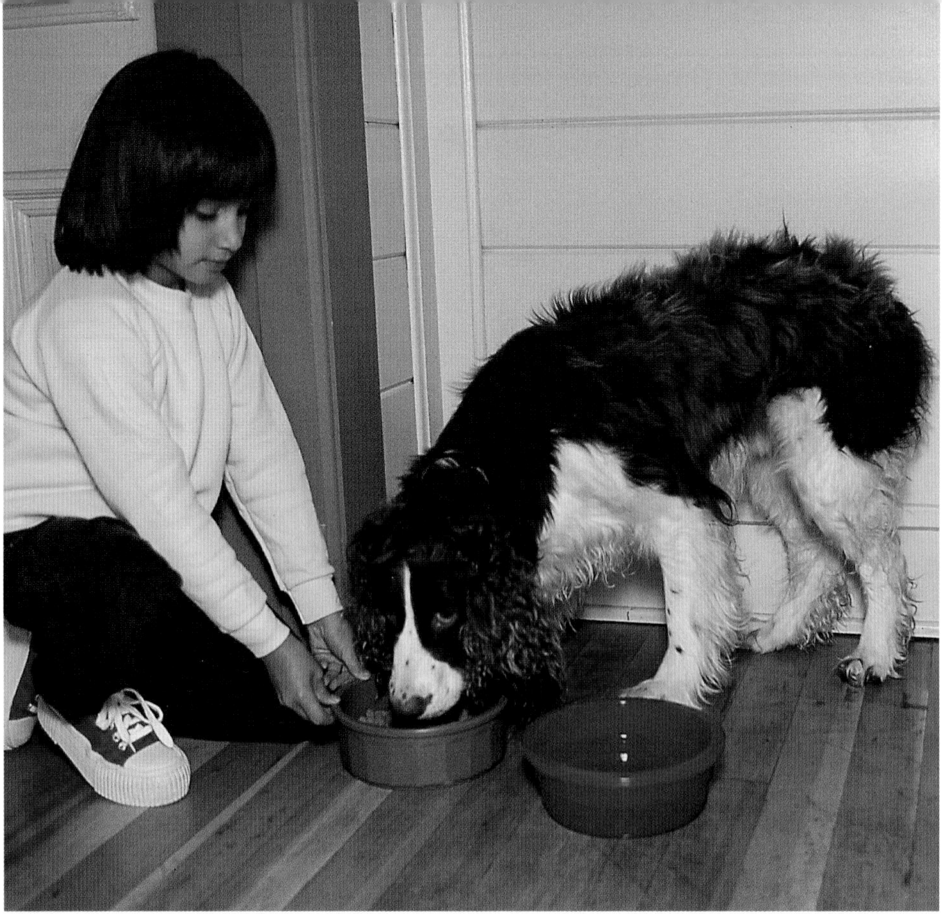

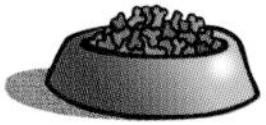

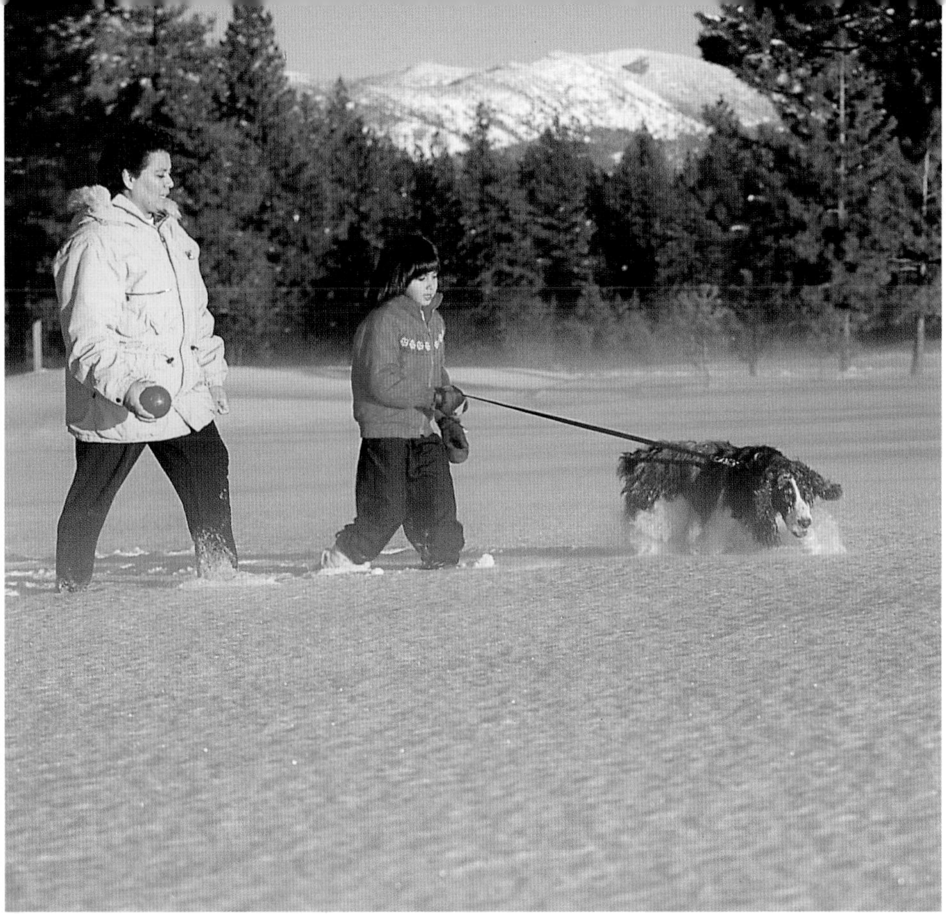

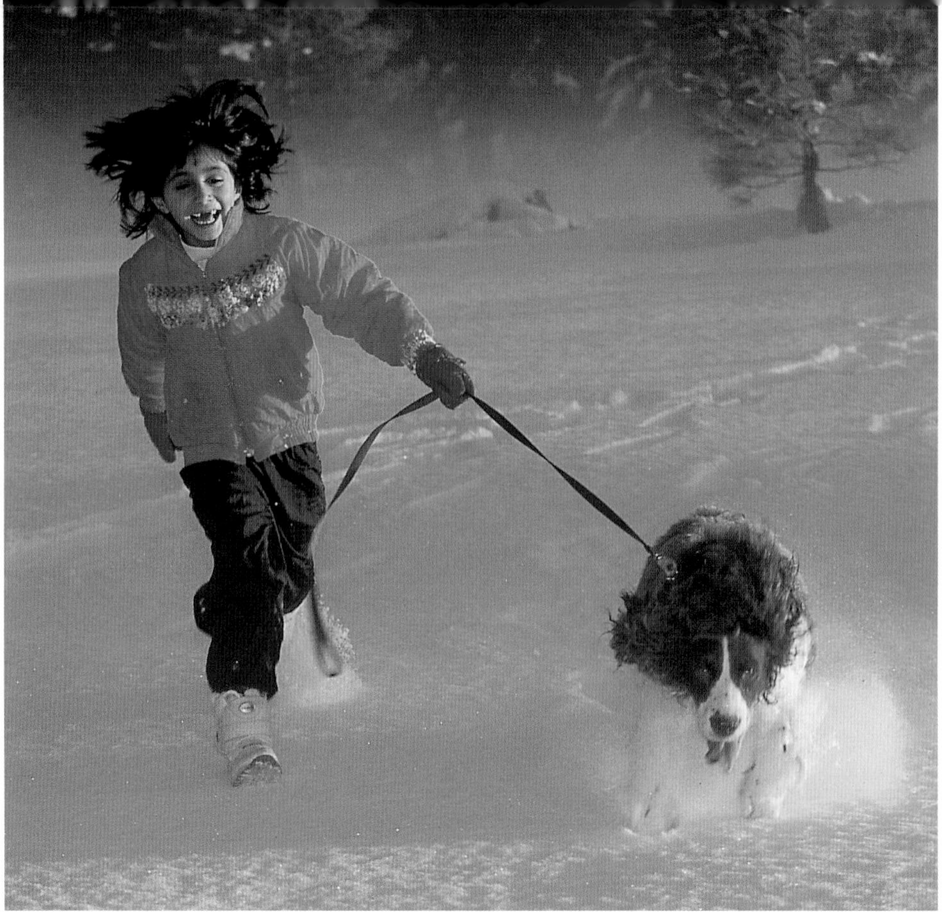

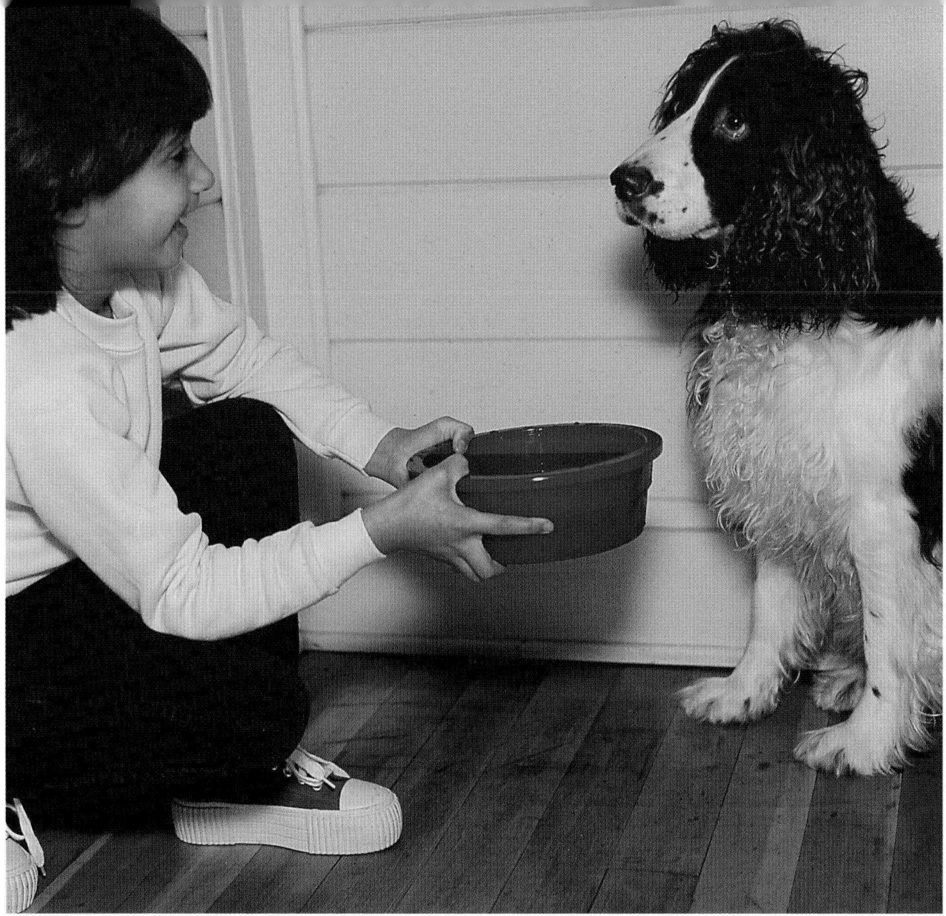

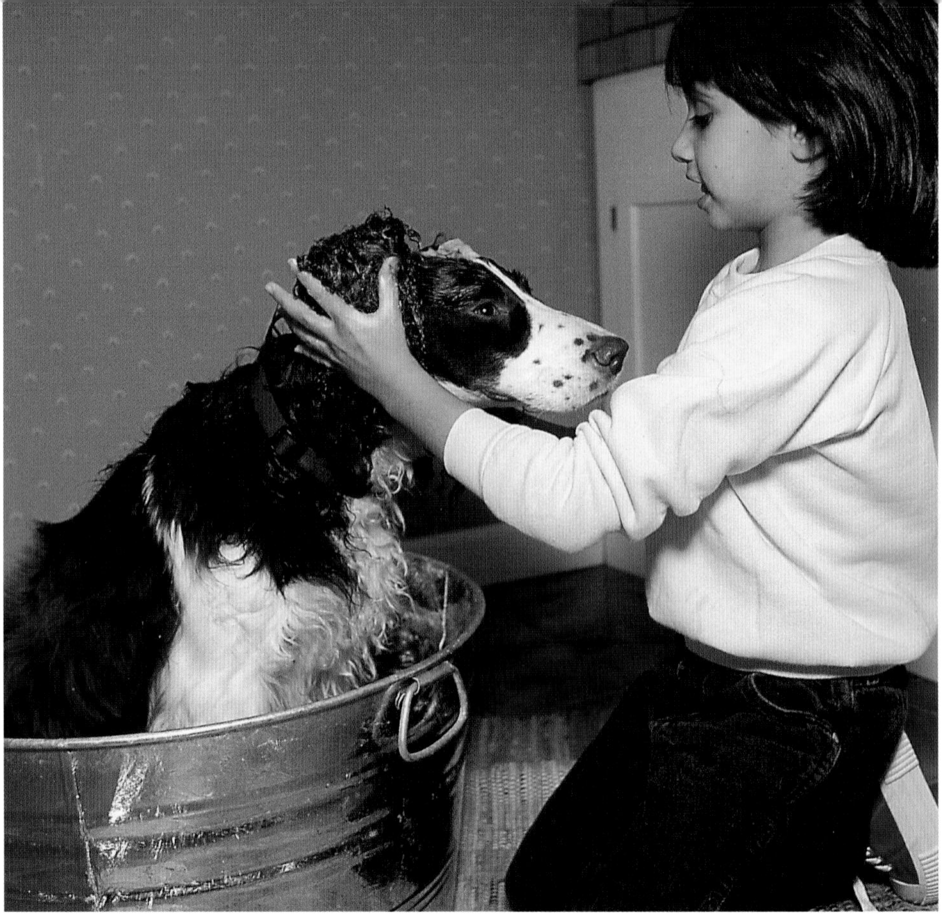

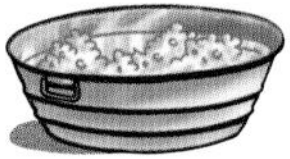

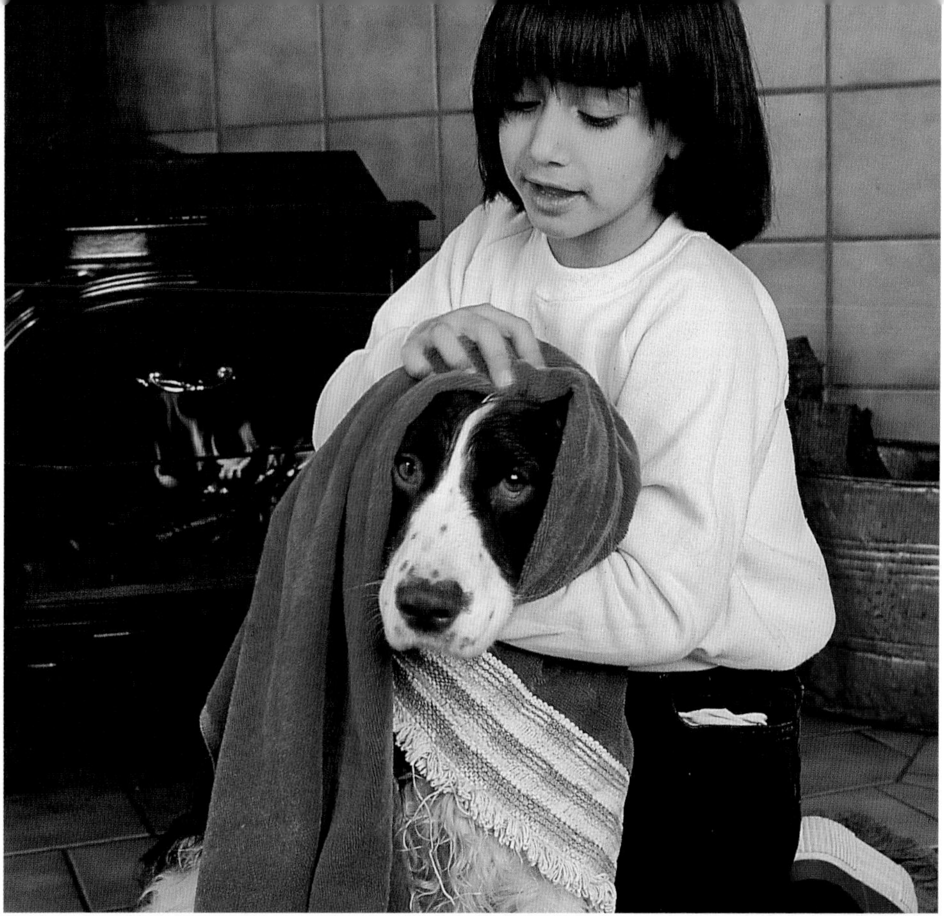

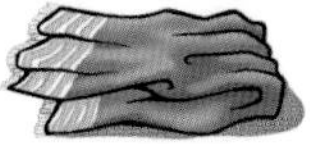

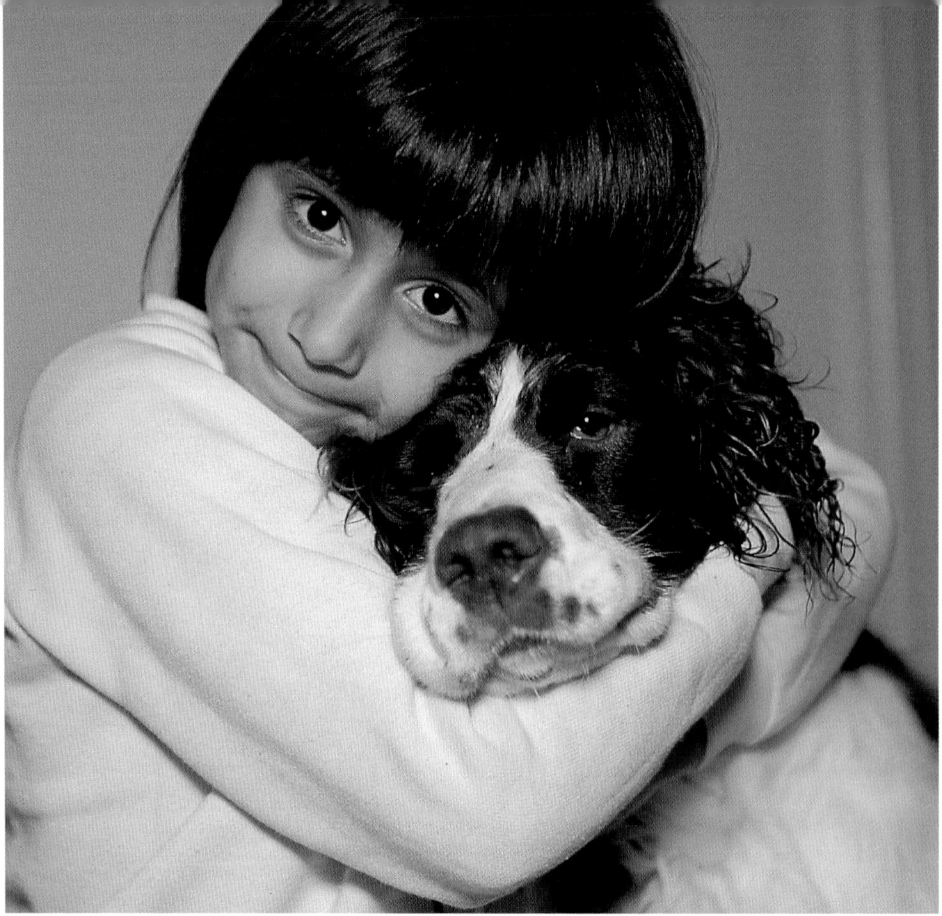